CW00750382

A PORTRAIT OF
CAMBRIDGE

DAGUR GUNNARSSON

A PORTRAIT OF
CAMBRIDGE

EDDA UK

A PORTRAIT OF CAMBRIDGE

Design and layout: Margrét E. Laxness

Printed in Slovenia

ISBN 1-904945-04-X

Introduction

Cambridge is known throughout the world as one of England's most famous university cities, dating back over 2000 years when the Romans established a settlement on a small hill north of the River Cam.

Today students come from every corner of the world to study a vast range of subjects at Cambridge University, from illuminated manuscripts to the hi-tech engineering of spacecrafts. During term-time the students and their professors can be seen whizzing about on their bicycles, which is still considered to be the best way to travel around the city.

The diversity of Cambridge itself is seen through the architectural splendour of its buildings, from the Saxon tower of St Bene't's, the oldest building in Cambridgeshire dating back to 1025, to the modern and futuristic award-winning buildings of the Isaac Newton Institute for Mathematical Sciences.

The market square in central Cambridge is the bustling hub of the city, where you can have your bicycle repaired, buy seasonal fruit, herbs and spices, hats and watches or simply spend some time watching people go about their business. As well as all the splendid college grounds and their chapels that are open to the public there are many interesting museums and art galleries waiting to be explored by curious visitors.

Cambridge, which received a charter giving city status in 1951, has something to please everyone and will never cease to amaze as the photographs in this book prove. The splendour of the Backs covered with spring flowers, the golden colour of the leaves forming a rich carpet in autumn, the cold crisp winter days and the glinting sun on the spires of King's College chapel make Cambridge a city for all seasons. Today, Cambridge welcomes over four million visitors a year, is home to 17,000 students and over 110,000 residents.

Cambridge is famous internationally for the Cambridge v Oxford boat race dating back to 1829 when students from St. John's College Cambridge challenged students from Oxford, affectionately known as "the other place," to a boat race which still takes place each year on the River Thames in London at Easter time. The River Cam, from which Cambridge gets its name, is ever popular today especially for the well-known pastime of punting along the Backs – the art of using a pole to push a flat-bottomed boat along whilst the passengers lay back and enjoy the view of the "back sides" of the privileged colleges who share the river banks.

The collection of images within this wonderful book gives a brief overview of some of the highlights of Cambridge: the many splendid buildings, the peaceful college gardens and open spaces, the river and medieval cobbled streets all encouraging you to turn to the next page whilst reluctantly moving away from the photograph facing you. To show the many facets of the city several books would be needed but this certainly whets the appetite and I am proud to put my name to what shows a brief insight to Cambridge, one of the world's best known cities.

Frankie McGhee

Tourism Business Manager, Visit Cambridge

1 The Warwick Vase on the lawn in front of Senate House is a bronze copy of a
second-century marble Roman urn once owned by Hadrian.

2 Senate House is the main building of The University of Cambridge.
This is where degrees are conferred on students.

3 Senate House by King's Parade.

4 Graduates from King's College on their way to a graduation ceremony at Senate House.

5 Top hats and capes are de rigueur for the porters on graduation day.

6 Walking on the lawns of the Cambridge colleges is a privilege enjoyed only by the dean or the head of the college, fellows and their guests.

7 Flower urns at Downing College.

8 Downing College; the architect William Wilkins was much influenced
by classical Greek architecture.

9 The nineteenth-century Grecian buildings of Downing College.

10 A door at the east range of Downing College. Notice the boot scrapers on either side.

11 Tourists from all over the world flock to Cambridge in all weathers.

12 The bicycle plays an important role in Cambridge and even if some of the street musicians

are rubbish they still liven up the streets.

13 The Eagle is famous for the graffiti on the ceiling of the Air Force Bar.

14 British pubs are unique institutions and there are quite a few to be found in Cambridge.

15 During the summer the streets and the river are alive with the hustle and bustle of people enjoying all the city has to offer.

16 Cambridge welcomes quite a few tourists throughout the year.

17 The bicycle is the best way to get around town.

18 Street musicians give passers-by an extra spring in their step.

19 Not everyone chooses to navigate the river in the traditional punt.

20 Sport is an essential part of college life in Cambridge.

21 A wealth of green on the Backs leading to King's College.

22　A detail of the water fountain of the Great Court at Trinity College.

23　The Great Court at Trinity College is the largest of its kind in both Cambridge and Oxford.

It was laid out at the end of the sixteenth century by Thomas Nevile, the then Master of the college.

24 Trinity College Dining Hall is the largest of its kind in Cambridge with a hammer beam ceiling and a large portrait of its founder, Henry VIII.

25 Decorated screen above the entrance to the dining hall.

26 Main entrance to Trinity College and the Great Court with one

of Cambridge's many sundials.

27 Edward III founded a college called King's Hall in 1336, which was united with another college,

Michaelhouse, to form Trinity College in 1546.

28 The porters at Trinity College still wear the traditional bowler hat;

Mr James Mackie wears his proudly.

29 The Wren library holds many treasures, illuminated manuscripts and early editions of Shakespeare,
poetry by Milton, Newton's personal papers and the original manuscript of Winnie the Pooh.
30 Nevile's Court with semi-classical cloisters was originally open to the river but in 1676 a library designed
by Sir Christopher Wren closed the court.

31 The colonnaded portico of the Fitzwilliam Museum.

32 The colonnade underneath the Wren Library of Trinity College, allowing passage to the river.

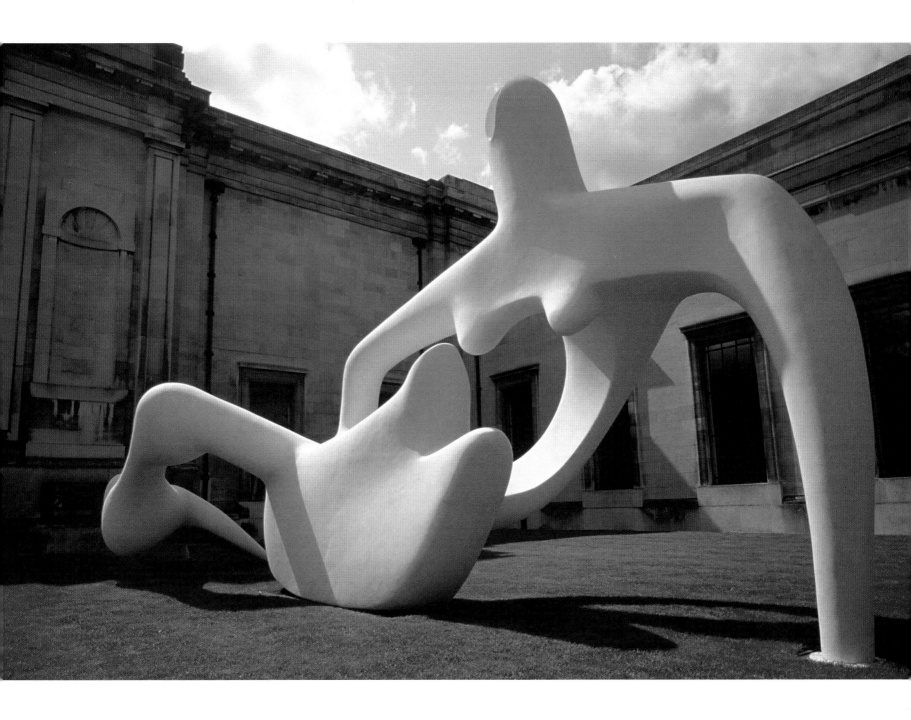

33 Lions guarding the entrance to the Fitzwilliam Museum that displays the University's magnificent collection of art and antiquities.

34 Henry Moore's Reclining Figure in painted plaster from 1951 in front of the Fitzwilliam Museum.

35 Interior of the modern part of Kettle's Yard, a house built in 1956 by Helen and Jim Ede, the former curator of the Tate Gallery in London. It now belongs to the University of Cambridge and houses the Edes collection of twentieth-century art

36 Kettle's Yard with the Saxon Church of St Peter's on Castle Hill in the background.

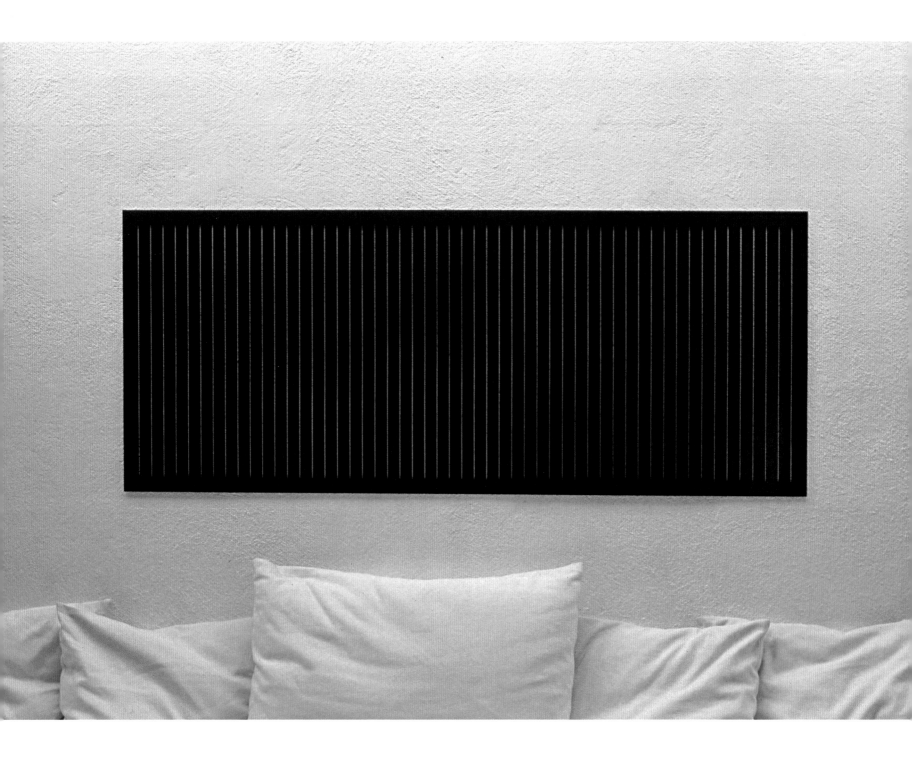

37 Douglas Allsop's Reflective Editor from 2003 was temporarily on display
in the extension downstairs at Kettle's Yard.

38 The magnifying lens dangling in front of the plants is a work by Gregorio Vardanega
entitled "Disk" from circa 1960.

39 Helen and Jim Ede picked the pebbles up on their seaside walks and arranged
them to resemble a Buddhist Mandala, both a representation of the universe and
an object of contemplation.

40 The narrow boat Nautilus moored by Jesus Lock.

41 Swans frequent the river Cam. Most of the swans living on Britain's waterways belong to and have been protected by the Crown since the twelfth century.

42 Clare College Bridge with its picturesque balls, one of them famously incomplete.

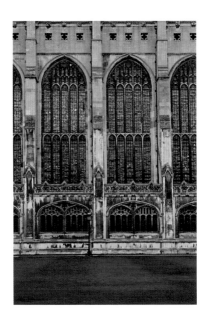

43 The south façade of King's College Chapel.

44 Clare College next to King's College Chapel.

45 The façade of King's College Chapel.

46 A porter on duty at King's College main entrance.

47 The gothic King's College Chapel versus the neo-classical neighbour of Clare College.

48 The grandiose fan-vaulted ceiling of King's College Chapel with its medieval stained-glass

windows and centrepiece organ.

The organ was built in 1605 – 1606 by Thomas Dalham.

49 A common sight in Cambridge.

50 The east end of King's College Chapel and the nineteenth-century stone screen.

51 The Market Square and Great St Mary's.

52 The colourful wares at the stalls of Market Square.

53 The first floor window display of Ryder and Amies who sell gowns to the scholars.

54 Ryder and Amies, also a popular shop with the tourists on King's Parade.

55 A tomb nestling next to St Bene't's (aka St Benedict's). The church tower, which dates from
Saxon times, was built in 1025 and is the oldest building in Cambridgeshire.
56 Great St Mary's, the University Church, in central Cambridge.

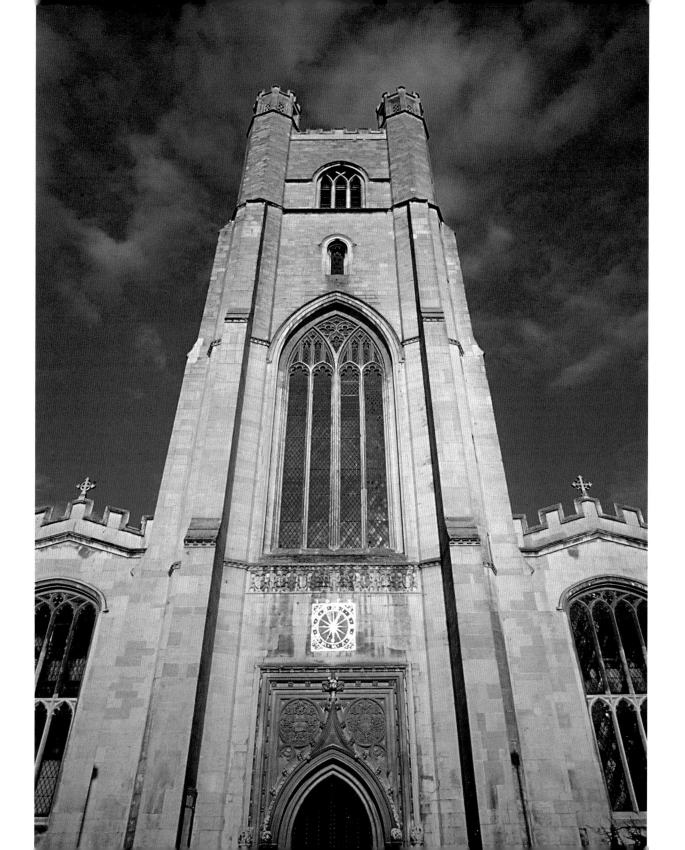

57 The Church of the Holy Sepulchre on Bridge Street is of a twelfth-century Norman design and is popularly known as the Round Church.

58 Our Lady and the English Martyrs Catholic Church was built in the Neo-Gothic style in the late nineteenth century.

59 Gargoyles hide in nooks and crannies in Cambridge.

60 Not all gargoyles are terrifying.

61 Cobbled streets, Senate House Passage and Cambridge University Library.

62 Chimneys at Trinity Lane.

63 A tombstone in front of St Mary the Less, better known as Little St Mary's Church on Trumpington Street. The church was originally the chapel of Peterhouse College.

64 St Peter's on Castle Hill is a tiny church from Saxon times.

65 The University Library built in 1931–34, designed by Giles Gilbert Scott, who is also famous for designing power stations and the classic red telephone box.

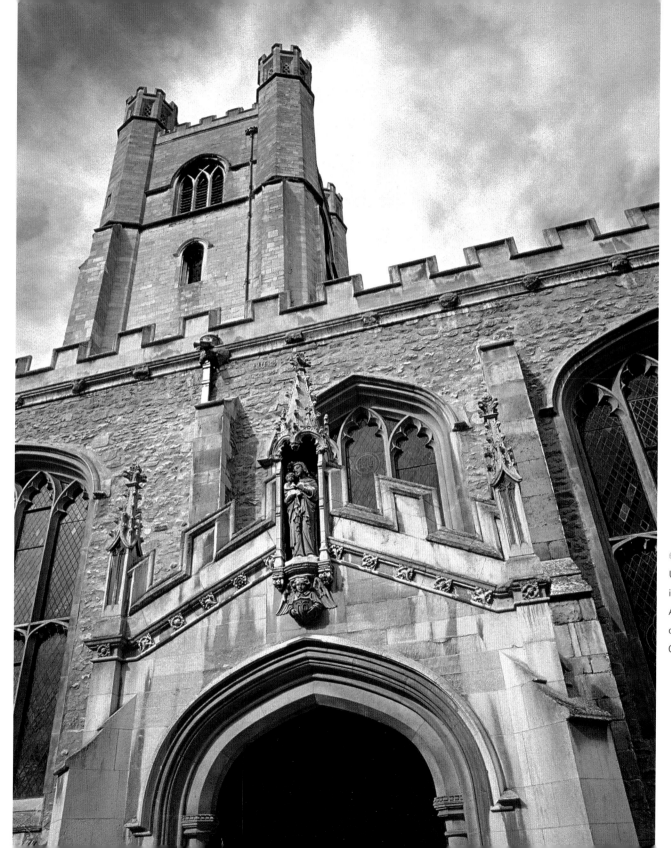

66 Great St Mary's, the University church, built in the fifteenth century. A climb up the tower offers a lovely view of Cambridge.

67 Early spring and no leaves on the trees but Christ's Pieces is still beautiful.

68 A small tower on Magdalene College.

69 Cambridge has attractive open spaces. The Jesus Green in early spring.

70 The artistic way to park a bike.

71 A rare painted gargoyle at Christ's College.
72 Bears guard the entrance to the Sedgwick Museum of Earth Sciences at
the University's Downing Site.

73 The Gate of Honour at Gonville and Caius College sports six sundials.
Graduates only pass through it on their way to receive their degrees at
Senate House.

74 A sign chalked on a wall at Senate House Passage leading tourists
to the river. The narrow passages in Cambridge can be confusing to a
newcomer; note the punting symbol to the right.

75 The local swan population frequents the lock.

76 The weeping willow forms a protective shield over the narrow boats moored at Jesus Lock.

77 A romantic bridge crossing the River Cam on the grounds of King's College.

78 Little Trinity, student accommodation on Jesus Lane built 1725.

79 The Jesus Green is a lovely place for a stroll.

80 Punting is a traditional pastime in Cambridge.

81 A quiet stretch of the river Cam, flowing past Darwin College. Punting is a tranquil and different way of enjoying the city, especially if you let a professional do all the hard work. It is not as easy as it looks.

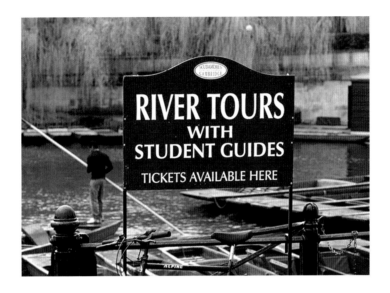

82 The Anchor Pub by the Mill Pool and the Silver Street Bridge.

83 Some student guides famously invent and embellish stories to amuse their
passengers as they glide along the River Cam in their punts.

84 On sunny days the river is quite an attraction.

85 Eager punters resemble medieval jousters with long lances on the Mill Pool by the
Silver Street Bridge.

86 A punt tout on the lookout for potential clients.

87 In summer it gets busy outside The Anchor and around the berth for the punts at the Mill Pool.

88 The Wooden Bridge is the proper name of this famous structure popularly known as Mathematical Bridge.

89 The original bridge was built in 1749. This is the second replacement which was constructed in 1905.

90 The sixteenth-century Queen's College Hall was redecorated in the eighteenth century and then restored in the nineteenth century with much of the work done by the firm of William Morris. The artistic-looking ghost is simply a passing tourist.

91 The President's Lodge above the fifteenth-century cloisters in 1911 the plaster covering the building was removed to uncover the Tudor half-timbering.

92 The cloisters of St John's New Building from 1831.

93 The Neo-Gothic New Building of St John's College represents a romantic Victorian view of the
Middle Ages with its cloisters and the central tower decorated with battlements and turrets.

94 Architectural details and gargoyles of Our Lady and the English Martyrs.

95 The cloistered front of the New Building of St John's College.

96 The Bridge of Sighs from 1831 connecting the New Building and the Backs with the older part of
the college. The name comes from a bridge in Venice which in turn gets its name from the
fact that it led to a prison.

97 Interior of the Bridge of Sighs and beyond it the cloisters of the New Building.

98 Details from the Senior Combination Room which is still only lit by candlelight.

99 The Senior Combination or Common Room is the longest one in Cambridge, 28 m long with a famous plaster ceiling and panel work. During the Second World War the D-Day landings were planned in part from this room.

ST. JOHN'S COLLEGE
ADMISSION CHARGES

ADULTS	£2.20
CHILD (12-16)	£1.30
SENIOR CITIZENS	£1.30
STUDENTS	£1.30
FAMILY TICKET	£4.40

PLEASE FOLLOW
THE VISITOR ROUTE
INDICATED ON YOUR
GUIDE TICKET

Cambridge Residents &
Members of the University
may enter free of charge

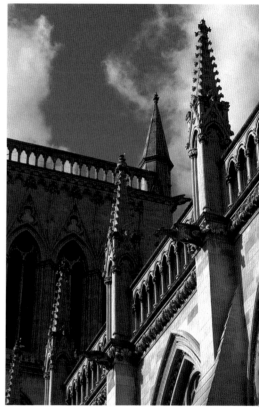

100 The gatehouse of St John's College with the coat of arms of Lady Margaret
Beaufort, the founder of the college and the mother of Henry VII.
101 Details of the chapel of St John's College; it was designed by Sir George Gilbert
Scott in 1869.

102 Architectural detail from St John's New Building.

103 A glassless stone window of St John's Third Court next to the Bridge of

Sighs and overlooking the River Cam.

104 A view from inside the cloisters of the New Building of St John's College towards the Bridge of Sighs.

105　The New Building of St John's College with a central cupola often referred to as
"The Wedding Cake".

106 A statue of Henry VIII on the side wall of the Wilkins' Building of King's College, facing King's Parade.

107 Bust of
Bartholomew Wortley
a long time fellow of
Caius College (d. 1749).
The bust is on the west
face of the Waterhouse
Building and can be seen
from the Senate House
Passage.

108 Gas lighting can still be found dotted around Cambridge.

109 The beautiful terraced houses of Orchard Street.

110 Narrow boats on the River Cam underneath a pedestrian bridge by the

College Boathouses.

111 Stacks of punts on dry land.

112 Bicycle repair shop behind the Anchor Pub by Silver Street.

113 A different kind of bicycle repair shop floating on the River Cam.

114 An example of Tudor half-timbering at Magdalene College.

115 Many students don the straw boaters and tout for punts. This one worked the beat on Bridge
Street which has a couple of charming Tudor houses.

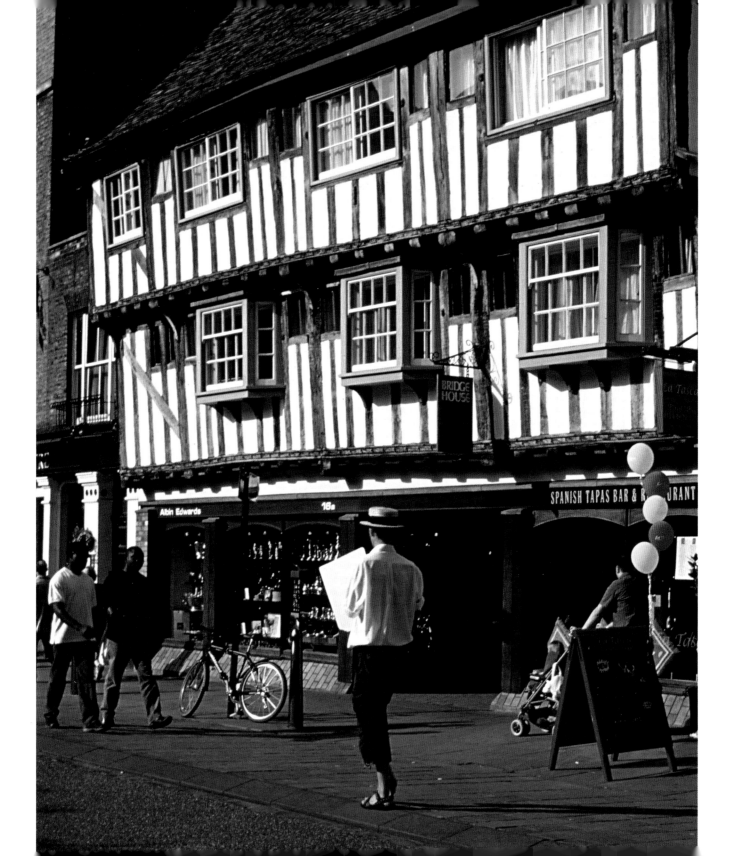

116 Rowing is a popular sport at Cambridge.

117 The summer sees two competitions called the Bumps. One is for the college students
and another for the townspeople. A small cannon is fired and each team tries to catch or
"bump" the team placed ahead of them on the river.

118 The team of the St Radegund Public House managed to bump another team and therefore get to wear impromptu laurels of willow and celebrate with a pint.

119 A team of eight with their cox at the Town Bumps.

120 The fountain at The Cambridge University Botanic Garden.

121 A cosy retreat in the Botanic Garden.

122 Black Pine (Pinus nigra salzmannii) in Cambridge University Botanic Garden. It was planted along the
main avenue in 1846 by Professor J. S. Henslow who was Darwin's mentor.

123 An example of old-fashioned beehives.

124 This apple tree is reputed to be a descendant of the tree which inspired Newton to write the
Laws of Gravitation.

125 The Betty and Gordon Moore Library at the Centre for Mathematical Sciences.

126 The Centre for Mathematical Sciences built in 2000-2001.

127 The Master's Lodge in the First Court at Christ's College.

128 A bust of John Milton who came up in 1628 and famously spent some time underneath a
mulberry tree in The Fellows' Garden writing poetry

129 The Fellows' Garden at Christ's College.

130 An eighteenth-century bathing pool, it is probably the oldest private bathing pool in the
country; records first mention it in 1763..

134 A temperance statue and the garden at Wolfson College.

135 Wolfson College.

136 Topiary in a privat garden.

137 The Old Court at Selwyn College.

138 The modern architecture of Churchill College built in 1960 on the outskirts of Cambridge.

139 The college is the national and Commonwealth memorial to Sir Winston Spencer Churchill (1874 - 1965).

140 The main gate of St Catharine's College.

141 The emblem of Catharine of Alexandria who was condemned to be crucified on a wheel. It miraculously broke when she touched it and she was beheaded instead and later canonised as a martyr of her faith.

142 Modern gargoyles.

143 An angel guarding a window of Our Lady and the English Martyrs the Catholic Church on Hills Road.

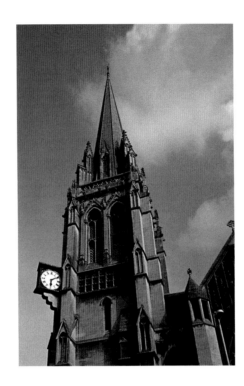

144 The clock tower of Our Lady and the English Martyrs Catholic Church on Hills Road.

145 A view of Our Lady and the English Martyrs from the grounds of Downing College.

Cambridge

Cambridge is brimming with history. If you take a stroll around the centre at a leisurely pace you will soon discover what this city is all about. The beautiful architecture fires the imagination, the old college courts with their immaculate and sacred lawns, turrets and chapels evoke a deep sense of history. And yet this famous seat of learning does not feel like a large museum or a collection of ruins, it is a busy bustling university city that continues to be at the forefront of academic and scientific achievements.

Central Cambridge is sufficiently large for the casual visitor to lose himself wandering among its many narrow lanes and shopping streets. That is part of the allure of the place, while it also makes it quite difficult finding again that charming little cheese shop or that curious antiquarian bookseller with the bookshelves on the outside of the shop.

An outing on the river is an excellent way of enjoying Cambridge. You could take a guided tour with a fresh-faced student at the helm of a punt giving you what may or may not be historically correct facts about the college buildings lining the river Cam, or, for those feeling confident enough, charter a punt and test one's skills in propelling a shallow boat with a very long stick - no doubt amusing bystanders with graceful flailing of arms in order to stay on board.

Newton, Milton, Wordsworth, Byron, Wittgenstein, the list goes on. They all roamed the streets of Cambridge at one time or another and it is not difficult to picture them here as so many things have remained unchanged for centuries.

Although the University, with its many beautiful colleges, is of course the main reason for most people's visits and has been for the past eight hundred years or so, Cambridge started out as a market town. Indeed, it was well placed at a crossroads between the Thames Valley and the Norfolk coast and most importantly, at a convenient site to ford the navigable river.

The name

Traces of early settlements from neolithic times have been discovered in Cambridge. The river offered means of transportation and a bridge across it eventually gave the town its name. The Roman name for Cambridge was most likely "Durolipons," a name that does not exactly roll off the tongue and therefore only lasted four or five centuries. In the Middle Ages the river was called Granta. And from the ninth to the thirteenth century the name of the town thus became Grantebryege which means "The Bridge across the river Granta" in Old Norse. Not to be confused with Grantchester, the hometown of the poet Rupert Brook, not far from Cambridge. "Cantebrig" is a version of the name in twelfth century sources and the modern version of the name first appeared in the fifteenth century.

Romans built a road from Colchester that led through Cambridge and further north to the outer extremities of the Roman Empire. They also built a wooden bridge near today's Magdalene Street Bridge and a small fortress on Castle Hill.

Later, Normans built a new fort on the old Roman site as a defence against the Saxons who came from the Fens. Another settlement rose across the river near Bene't Street, so for a while Cambridge consisted of two villages on opposite sides of the river. Since this was the only convenient place to cross the river for miles and with the Fens forming another natural barrier to the east, traffic flowed through Cambridge and trading was brisk. A small river harbour was built and the town prospered.

In 1010 the affluent town was plundered and destroyed by an invading Viking force. The Vikings did not linger long in historic terms and Cambridge was quickly rebuilt and by 1066 it was again a thriving market town.

In 1068 William the Conqueror visited Cambridge on his way back from peace talks in Scotland. He had a castle built on Castle Hill on the same site as the older fortifications. If you walk up to the top of the hill you will see why it is such a good spot for defence. From there you can see the surrounding terrain for many miles and a surprise attack would be virtually impossible.

Town and Gown

In the early thirteenth century, students fled the riots in Oxford; some of them came to Cambridge and formed what we know today as the University. Peterhouse, the first college, was founded in 1284 by the Bishop of Ely. This was followed by Clare College, originally known as University Hall, and by Pembroke in the early fourteenth century. Today, Cambridge has 31 colleges, eight University Museums and numerous university buildings, all interspersed among shops, offices and residential housing, giving a harmonious mix of town and gown working and living together.

But that was not always the case, as very early on the students complained about high prices and being charged for both food and lodging by the locals. The King backed the University and in 1231 Henry III forbade the town's people to overcharge the scholars for goods and rent. This caused friction between town and gown that went on for centuries. In the fourteenth century every new mayor of Cambridge had to swear an oath to maintain the privileges of the University. The town's people called it the Black Assembly. As the University grew in size, matters were reversed, as the University acquired land and buildings and became the town's principal landlord.

A peasant's revolt in 1381 escalated into a general uprising against the University. In a ceremony in the market place the mayor forced the scholars to give up their privileges. They were required to sign a document stating that they would obey the rules of the town and that the townspeople would from now on determine the price of things. The King would have none of this and by royal decree the University decided from then on the prices of food and drink and regulated weights and measures. Both the town and the University spent an enormous amount of time and money bickering about rights and pleading with the authorities.

There were also long spells of calm and quiet and today things tend to be calm on the town and gown front but skirmishes were erupting well into the middle of the twentieth century.

Parliament finally set an act in 1856 abolishing the Black Assembly and the University's right to supervise ale houses, markets and fairs as well as weights and measures.

The Colleges

The first colleges were originally built in response to a need for lodgings for the students and their tutors, who started to arrive in droves as the reputation of the University grew. Soon after Peterhouse was formed other colleges were created, and a century later seven colleges were up and running. After two more centuries there were twelve. The main subjects taught were Theology, Law and Latin. Needless to say only boys were admitted and at around 14-years-old they were younger than today's students. To gain admission to the University they were required to know how to read and write and to master the basics of Latin. Some of the colleges were based on religious establishments that were dissolved for one reason or other; Jesus, Christ's and St. John's, for instance.

In 1594 decline set in and both the University and the town experienced the slump. No new colleges were formed for more than two hundred years. It was not until the late nineteenth century that a glorious new era began, with new buildings erected and the formation of the first women's colleges (Girton in 1869 and Newnham in 1872). Still, degrees were not conferred on women until 1948 and attempts to make women full members of the University were repeatedly defeated until 1947.

Royalty has played an important role in the history of Cambridge. Both Henry VI and Henry VIII founded colleges – King's in 1441 and Trinity in 1546.

Lady Margaret Beaufort (1443 - 1509) was the influential mother of Henry VII and was not only instrumental in bringing an end to the disastrous War of the Roses but also formed two colleges in Cambridge. The oddly named God's House was demolished and reformed as Jesus College on a new site in 1505 and in her will Lady Beaufort left a provision for the founding of St. John's College. Before she died she began the work of turning the hospital of St. John the Evangelist (founded in the eleventh century) into a college for students of the Liberal Arts and Theology.

King's College

King's College is undoubtedly the most famous of all the colleges, mostly due to its beautiful and world famous chapel. The college was a pet project of the young Henry VI. His plans were on a grander scale than Cambridge had seen up until then, as he wanted the college and its buildings to reflect his greatness as a ruler. The 12 students were to be exclusively drawn from Eton College which he had founded a few years earlier. Henry VI was a religious man and he chose the number 12 because that was the number of the Apostles, later he altered his plans and 70 students entered the college. He went to great lengths to ensure that the chapel would be the greatest building of its kind. He even drew up detailed instructions for the construction of the grand new part of the college himself, but magnificent as those plans were, the chapel was the only building ever completed and even that took a century to build. The foundation stone of the chapel was laid in 1446 but when the King was deposed in 1461 the building work ground to a halt. Up until then the stonemasons had worked in magnesium limestone from Yorkshire. When work continued in 1476 they used sandstone from Northamptonshire. It took four more kings to finish the chapel. Both Edward IV and Richard III contributed funds to keep the construction going and by then it was largely roofed and almost ready. Construction then stopped until Henry VII provided the funds to fit the chapel out with its splendid and unequalled fan-vaulted

ceiling but this was completed only after his death in 1515. The chapel was finally ready for use in 1544 when Henry VIII had donated funds for the rood screen, the stalls in the choir and most importantly the wonderful stained-glass windows.

The final addition came in 1961 when the east end of the chapel was radically altered to accommodate Rubens's painting of the Adoration of the Magi which was presented to the college by the late Major A.E. Allnatt. It was painted in 1631 for the Convent of the White Nuns at Louvain in Belgium.

A Local Son

Oliver Cromwell was born in nearby Huntingdon in 1599. He was an undergraduate of Sidney Sussex College and later represented Cambridge in Parliament and had much influence in the area. Cromwell was a Puritan and led the Parliamentarians against the Royalists in the English Civil War of 1642 – 1647. Most of the constituents backed Cromwell, their MP, whereas the colleges had royal backing and were therefore Royalist. When Charles I lost the Civil War, his throne and finally his head on a cold January day in 1649, bad times were to follow for the colleges in Cambridge.

Cromwell became Lord Protector in 1653, he died in 1658 and in 1661 was posthumously executed and his tarred head placed on a flagpole on the Houses of Parliament. After the skull blew down in a storm it passed from one private collector to another until it was finally interred at a secret location in or near the chapel at his old college, Sydney Sussex College as late as 1960.

Cambridge has seen many great minds at work, for instance William Harvey who discovered the circulation of the blood in 1628 and Isaac Newton who worked to give explanation to gravity in Cambridge in 1687. Charles Darwin described the mechanism of evolution in 1859, Ernest Rutherford along with Cockcroft and Walton split the atom in 1932, Crick and Watson discovered the structure of DNA in 1953 and Professor Stephen Hawking, a current resident, wrote the surprise best-seller A Brief History of Time in 1988.

Numerous poets and famous writers have been educated at Cambridge, not to mention the infamous spies Maclean, Burgess, Philby and Blunt who were all at Trinity.

Christopher Marlowe, John Milton, Lord Byron and E.M. Forster all studied at Cambridge to name a few famous writers. Alfred, Lord Tennyson and Sylvia Plath also graced Cambridge with their presence. Latter-day authors who attended the University include P.D. James, Salman Rushdie and Nick Hornby.

Modern Cambridge

In 1845 the railway reached Cambridge and the scholars saw to it that the station was built as far away from the city centre and the colleges as possible. This modern invention was considered to be far too noisy and disruptive to be installed anywhere near serious-minded academics.

After 1851 sport became a notable part of college life. The Oxford and Cambridge Boat Race and the inter-university cricket matches had already begun as early as 1827, and became annual events in 1839. Boat clubs and other athletic organisations were formed and regular competitions between the colleges became a feature of undergraduate life. Until 1970, gowns had to be worn on the streets after dark by all junior members, and colleges closed their gates well before midnight. This was meant to keep the students in check and out of trouble in town.

The number of undergraduates increased dramatically after World War II when female students were allowed full membership and by the foundation of a third women's college, New Hall (1954), as well as the foundation of Churchill (1960) and Robinson (1977). In the 1960s four new colleges were established to provide fellowships for the growing number of teaching and research staff, more places were also added for research students. The older colleges also began to admit women students and appoint women fellows. These days all colleges admit women, but three colleges admit women students only - Newnham, New Hall, and Lucy Cavendish.

These days Cambridge is a permanent fixture on the tourist circuit, day-trippers flock to the city all year round, drawn there by the beauty of its buildings and the richness of its history. The tourist industry is thriving and that in turn encourages further development of museums and helps to preserve the local heritage. The town and gown mentality is waning and the city has gained much by its close ties with the University; there are now many hi-tech industries in the area that have been set up in conjunction with research that originated at the University.

Cambridge has truly adapted well throughout the centuries. Today, it preserves its historic heritage splendidly while being at the forefront of developing modern technology and will, in all likelihood, continue to do so long into the future.

Acknowledgements

Photographs of King's College by kind permission of the Provost and Fellows of King's College, Cambridge.

Photographs of Christ's College by kind permission of the Master, Fellows and scholars of Christ's College Cambridge.

Photographs of Downing College by kind permission of the Master, Fellows and scholars of Downing College, Cambridge.

Photographs of St John's College by kind permission of the Master, Fellows and scholars of St John's College, Cambridge.

Photographs of Queen's College by kind permission of the President, Fellows and scholars of Queen's College, Cambridge.

Photographs of Trinity College by kind permission of the Master, Fellows and scholars of Trinity College, Cambridge.

Photographs from Cambridge University Botanic Garden by kind permission of the superintendent of the Garden.

Photographs of Kettle's Yard by kind permission of the Curator of Collections.

Thanks to:
The bursars, their secretaries and helpful porters at all the Cambridge University Colleges. To Emma Kemp and Linda French, Brynjólfur "Binni" Jónsson, Daniel Sambraus, Gary Wade, Ian Wilton, Kevin Quinn and family, Margrét Laxness, Olivia Sheringham, Terry at St Radegund's and the staff at Kettle's Yard.
A big thank you goes of course to Björn and Elísabet, the publishers of this book, for their support and belief in me as a photographer. Gunnþórunn Guðmundsdóttir who managed a sneaky cameo appearance deserves the biggest thanks because without her this book would not be in your hands.